Wood Pallet:

Redecorate Your House in No Time. Over 30 Projects With Easy and Detailed Instructions

All photos used in this book, including the cover photo were made available under a Attribution 2.0 Generic (CC BY 2.0) and sourced from Flickr.

Table of contents

Introduction 4
Chapter 1: Safety Precaution 15
Chapter 2 - Tools you need 17
Chapter 3 – Around the House 22
Chapter 4 – In the Garden 41
Chapter 5 – In the Garage 54
Chapter 4 – Storage and Decoration Ideas 58
Conclusion 74

Introduction

Wooden pallets can be a brilliant source of both materials and inspiration. With the current trend for a more rustic, reclaimed or recycling look, pallets fit in perfectly to the new style. When left unpainted, they have a pleasantly rustic, practical appearance, but will also take paint, stains or finishes extremely well, making them very versatile. For many people, the knowledge that they are re-using an existing material (rather than creating a demand for new resources to be used up) is a big part of their appeal.

Another big advantage of wooden pallets is that they can also be acquired relatively cheaply – and sometimes even free of charge!

If you live (or drive past) a business which gets heavy goods delivered (such as a building supply yard or wine merchants) the chances are good that their stock is delivered on pallets, and that they have more than they require. Ask them nicely if you can have or buy their pallets. Never 'just take' any pallets that you see lying around.

This is theft – some yards will recycle or sell on the pallets themselves and so, even if it looks as though the pallets are not being used, may take a dim view of someone helping themselves. Bear in mind as well that many yards have CCTV. It is much better to establish a friendly relationship with whoever owns the yard – this will make it easier to get a regular supply of pallets for future projects.

When selecting a business as a potential source of pallets, think about what sort of materials they transport. A business which deals with animal or pet feed is likely to use pallets which do not contain harmful chemicals. One which deals in industrial chemicals or imports fruit and vegetables from overseas is likely to have less safe pallets. Make it easier on yourself to find good, useable pallets.

If you don't have any likely local businesses, check the 'for sale' ads in a website for your area, such as Gumtree, Freecycle or Craigslist. You will probably find someone selling wooden pallets for low prices and they may even deliver them to your home.

If you want to buy brand new pallets (more on why you might find yourself wanting to do that below) then your best bet is to find a supplier on the internet. Bear in mind that they are unlikely to be interested in selling you one or two pallets, and may insist on quite a large order. If this is a case, ask around your friends and neighbors to see if any of them are interested in splitting an order with you. You may find that there is quite a bit of enthusiasm for pallet projects, once you explain what your plans are for your pallets.

Even if you are buying brand new pallets, check before you place your order that they have not been treated with any potentially harmful chemicals. You are looking for food safe pallets, particularly if you intend to use them for any projects which will bring them into contact with children, pets, food or vegetables intended for consumption.

One of the downsides of buying second hand pallets is that you do not know what they have been used to transport or treated with. Many will have been treated with pesticides, rodenticides and fungicides, and (despite all of these chemical nasties) could still be awash with germs.

The wood used for the pallets is often very porous and once it has become damp, can quickly become a breeding ground for bacteria. This risk is even greater if the pallet has been used to transport fruit and vegetables.

For this reason, many people choose not to use pallets for projects that will bring them into close contact with food, pets or children. Some people decide not to bring pallets into the house at all, reserving their use for the garden, and even avoiding keeping them near plants which are intended for consumption.

Always wear gloves when inspecting pallets for sale. Although these tips cannot **guarantee** that a pallet is safe to use, you should take the following precautions:

- Do not use a pallet that has obvious spill or stain marks on it. Pallet wood is extremely porous and you will not be able to clean off whatever the mystery spill is.

- Avoid pallets which have been used for the transportation of fruit and vegetables. They have a high chance of containing harmful bacteria.

- Check for bent or rusted nails holding the pallet together. These will make it harder to deconstruct. If there seem to be a lot of nails, not only will this spoil the look of your finished project, but may indicate that the pallet has been repaired or repurposed already. Similarly, don't choose ones with broken slats or missing pieces. You want good, sturdy pallets for your projects – there is no need to take ones which are already in poor condition.

- Look for wood which has the IPPC stamp. This is a mark that indicates that the wood has been treated to prevent it from carrying invasive plant or insect species. The wood can be treated in one of two ways, and will have been marked to indicate which:

- Method One: Heat treatment. The pallet will have been heated to at least 56 degrees for at least 30 minutes. The wood will be marked with 'HT' to indicate the use of this method.

- Method Two: Chemical fumigation. The wood will have been treated with a chemical called methyl bromide. It will be stamped with the letters 'MB'. Do **NOT** use any pallet that has been treated with methyl bromide – its use has been banned since 2010, but there are still pallets in circulation that were created before that date.

- You may also find the letters 'DB'. This indicates that the wood has been debarked and will not have been exposed to pesticides. This pallet can be considered safe to use.

The markings on the pallet may not be clear – if you are in any doubt, do not select that pallet for use. When selecting marked second hand pallets, do not choose ones which do not have the IPPC and HT/DB stamps on them.

However, the other option is to choose pallets which have no markings on at all. This indicates that they have only bee used for domestic transportation.

It is also a good idea to avoid pallets which have been painted. These are often used by the pool industry, and the likelihood that they have been exposed to dangerous chemicals is high. They may be initially appealing – they are often painted in bright blues or aquas, which have often faded and peeled to give a brilliant 'distressed' finish, but be strong and avoid them. You can recreate that finish at home safely, if you have the time and inclination.

Ultimately, there is always a slight risk associated with using second hand pallets, and there is no way of guaranteeing that they are 100 per cent safe. If you feel unhappy taking this risk, it is probably best to buy your pallets from new.

If you have bought a second hand pallet, you should clean it thoroughly before use. A pressure washer is ideal for this job, or you can scrub the pallet with hot soapy water. Allow it to dry outside and wear gloves while handling the pallet.

Remove the nails (if you are deconstructing the pallet). This can be a difficult job; especially if the nails are bent and rusted (this is something to check for before you purchase the pallet). You may find it easiest to drive the nails all the way through the wood (rather than levering them out, which may cause the wood to split or crack). Use a drift or a punch to force the nails out to the other side.

You can also cut through any stubborn nails using a circular saw. However, you should expect to lose a few planks to breakage when you are deconstructing a pallet. For this reason, always get a few spares when preparing for a project.

The wood used for pallets is often very rough and can be a risk of splinters. You may want to sand the wood before use to give a better look to your finished project, but bear in mind that part of the aesthetic of pallet projects is that the wood retains a certain rough-hewn, industrial quality. A light sanding to remove any extremely rough or dangerous areas and then a few layers of beeswax should give you a nice finish.

When sanding, make sure to wear respiratory protection, as any chemicals which may have soaked into the wood will be released into the atmosphere and may be breathed in.

You will need standard woodworking tools to create your pallet projects, and a reasonable level of competency in using them. Although working with pallets is (in the main) simple and straightforward, this is only in relation to cabinet-making.

If you have never used tools such as a circular saw or an electric sander before, it would be a good idea to either ask a more experienced friend to help you, or take a short beginner's class in basic woodworking. This is also a good way to find out if you enjoy woodwork, or have a natural flair for it. It is best to find this out before you invest a lot of money in power tools or a stack of pallets you then lose your enthusiasm for.

A word about burning pallets:

Remember that burning any unwanted offcuts (or even whole pallets) will release all of the chemicals that the wood has been treated with. If in any doubt, to not burn your offcuts, and certainly do not use it as a method of using up pallets which you have rejected for craft projects on the basis that they have been exposed to dangerous chemicals. The same goes for painted wood, especially old paint which may still contain lead.

Decorating Your Projects:

As previously discussed, you should avoid any pallets which have already been painted. However, the raw wood of the pallets make them extremely versatile for painting, staining, varnishing or leaving bare.

If you intent to use your pallet wood outside, then it is a good idea to treat it with something to help it withstand the weather. Pallet wood is very porous, and the rain will make it moulder quickly. This will also encourage the growth of bacteria. Likewise, heat and sunshine will cause the wood to dry out, warp and crack if it is not treated.

Purpose built outside furniture is usually constructed for a hardwood such as teak, redwood or cedar, and so you should not expect your pallet-built furniture to last as long as a standard outdoor bench or table.

Paint, by its very nature, is better at blocking UV rays than a clear finish, such as varnish, oil or wax. Before painting your project, you should sand the finish so that the primer adheres better, and use a quality outdoor primer. This will also help your paint to last longer.

Pick a paint which is designed for outdoor use. There is now a wide range of colours and finishes available for outdoor projects, so this should not restrict your creativity.

You should also regularly check your outdoor furniture for signs of wear, and give it a new coat of paint every year to prolong its life. Similarly, look for a varnish that is designed for outside use if you want to give the project a more natural finish.

For inside projects, you don't have to worry so much about protecting the wood. Small inside craft projects are a great way to use up left over or half full paint pots from decorating your house. Another advantage of this is that your new piece with naturally fit in with your existing colour scheme. However, there are a number of different techniques you might like to consider as well as just straightforward painting:

Adding a Wash:

This is very simple to do – you simply water down your existing paint. Rather than a thick, opaque layer, you are left with a pale, semi-transparent matt finish, which still shows the grain of the wood beneath. Experiment with different concentrations of paint on an off cut to make sure that you are happy with it, before slapping it on to your finished project.

Distressing:

The idea of this is to make the wood look old and as though it has been painted several times over its lifetime. You will need two different colours; a main colour and an undercoat. The greater the contrast between these two colours, the bolder the finished look will be.

Paint a layer of undercoat and allow to dry. Paint the topcoat, allow to dry and then add a layer of furniture wax. Using fine sandpaper, rub at areas such as corners and protuberances to remove the to coat and show the colour underneath. When you are happy with the look, apply another coat of wax to seal the paint.

Waxing:

This is a great way to bring out the natural beauty of the wood. This works best on pieces that already have a natural grain; it will be less effective on raw, featureless pine. Apply several thin coats of wax to the wood, allowing it to dry thoroughly in between, and then buff to a shine with a soft cloth. You can achieve a more aged 'dirty' appearance by using a darker wax on a paler wood.

Gilding:

You can buy loose sheets of gold foil (or brass, for a more economical project) which you then carefully brush onto glue to adhere it to your project. This creates a very glamorous finish, and less is definitely more when it comes to gilding.

Stenciling:

This is a great way to personalize an otherwise standard piece of furniture There is a huge range of stencils available, or you can make your own out of acetate or even thick wallpaper. Just use a craft knife to cut out where you want the paint to go. Stipple the paint carefully through the stencil, and remember that it doesn't have to be perfect. You can create a wonderful vintage look by sanding or fading out a simple pattern.

Decoupage:

This is a method of decoration that became popular in the Victorian period with the rise of printed materials. Images and colours cut from magazines, wallpaper and wrapping paper are layered onto objects and then varnished to seal. Despite being a Victorian technique, you can create some very modern looks by using striking images from magazines and advertising.

Makes sure you have plenty of material cut out and to hand before you start, and consider your design carefully before you begin gluing, as you will find it very hard to remove or adjust images which have already be stuck down. A matt varnish is best for sealing, as a glossy finish may reflect the light and obscure the images.

Many people who enjoy painting furniture recommend chalk paint, as it gives a great finish and does not not require priming. It is also suitable for indoor and outdoor use, which is helpful if you want to create a flow between interior and exterior areas of your home – for example, in a conservatory or on a sun porch. However, chalk paint is not the cheapest, and you may want to be sure that you have a project that you are really keen on in mind before you invest in a pot.

Chapter 1: Safety Precaution

You want to make sure that the pallets that you are using in your home wooden pallet projects are not ones that have been used to load dangerous contaminants or have signs that they are covered in bacteria. Just remember that if your wooden pallets have been kiln dried they will be marked with the HT for heat treated, these would be the best choice to use in your home projects.

Ways to Disassemble Wooden Pallets

You will find that wooden pallets tend to be pretty sturdy this could make them hard to disassemble. You can use a pry bar and hammer to help in separating the bottom rails from the top slats of your wooden pallet. Use the pry bar to wedge between and separate the bottom rails pieces from the slats, then take the claw of the hammer to remove the nails. You may find that this method for removing the nails is not only very time consuming but can result in damage to the wooden pallet as well.

There is other ways that you can choose to disassemble your wooden pallets one other way is using a saw commonly known as a 'Sawzall.' This is a reciprocating saw that can make the job easier for you. This type of saw has a blade that can cut through nails. You just need to pry the boards apart wide enough to insert the saw to cut the nails. This method of disassembling the pallet will preserve the whole pallet.

You can also choose to use a chain saw or circular saw to remove the wooden slats from the rails of your wooden pallet. You will end up with shorter pieces of wood. From a wooden pallet that is 42" you will probably be left with slats about 18" once you have cut them. You must also remember when using this method not to let the blade of your chain saw or circular saw touch the nails, this could damage your saw and also cause injury to you from a flying piece of metal.

Keep in mind the pallet wood is rough so you should make sure to wear safety glasses and work gloves when you are disassembling them.

Tips When Painting Wooden Pallets

It is great fun using wooden pallets to use in your home projects; just by painting them you can really transform the whole look of them. Before you begin painting your wooden pallets after disassembling them you should send them to avoid splinters as they are very rough. The best type of tool for this job is either a mouse or orbital sander. Make sure to sand the pallet completely, remove the dust with a damp cloth. Clean the pallet wood to make sure that the paint will adhere to it. The next step is to decide to prime or not to prime; pallets tend to be porous so this can give your paintjob a very uneven finish.

I would suggest that you prime your wood first before you begin painting. If you want to go for a more aged or rustic look then I would skip using the primer. You should have no problems with the paint adhering to the wood if it is dry' and porous, especially if it has been sanded. If you want your paint job to have and even finish then you should use the primer before you paint.

Chapter 2 - Tools you need

The tools of the trade of woodworking are numerous. You'll find anything from simple hand tools to large, boisterous power tools that could seriously injure you. It might be best to start out with hand tools only and move on to power tools when you're more comfortable with woodworking. Besides, working with hand tools will allow you to learn the texture of the wood and you'll be better at using the power tools when the time comes.

For beginners, I'm going to talk about hand tools first.

Hand Tools

There are hundreds of woodworking specific hand tools available to novices, but we're going to start with the basics that you can find at any hardware store.

Most of you know what a hammer is, but did you know there are different types of hammers? For woodworking, you need the traditional ball point hammer.

Screwdrivers

You're going to need various sizes and types of screwdrivers, so it's best to get a kit where there is a base handle with attachments for Philips, flatheads, and hex attachments just to be safe. Depending upon your projects, you're going to want very small screws such as eyeglass screws and larger ones for things like tables. So be sure you have the right screwdriver and attachment for the project.

Nails and Screws

It depends upon your project, but you may need nails or you may need screws to make your joints more secure or attach pieces together. There are hundreds of different nails and screws, so you have to be sure you have the correct ones for the project you're doing.

Chisels

Chisels come in all shapes and sizes. There are very tiny ones to create small grooves or to flatten out a tiny area, and then there are ones that you're going to need to use a hammer on the end of in order to get it to work Again, be sure you have the right size for your project. Better yet, get a kit.

Saws

Keyhole saws, crosscut saws, coping saws, and backsaws are just a few of the different types of handheld, manual saws you can buy. They all have a different use, so be sure you're using the correct one. Otherwise, you may end up hurting your project or yourself.

Speed Square

Nifty squares that not only tell you if something is square, but they have measurements so that you can be sure your parts are the proper lengths.

Clamps

Imperative to woodworking, you're going to need clamps in order to keep your joints together when you glue them.

Clamps come in all different sizes and there are several different types: spring loaded, bar, C-clamps, trigger clamps, and many more. Know which ones you're going to need for your project and use them accordingly.

Hand Plane

There are numerous different kinds of planes available, and all of them are used in woodworking. Sometimes you can get away with not using a plane, but they're really handy to have available when you have an uneven thickness in a piece of wood.

If you're working with a raw piece of wood, meaning it's a log, you're going to need a hand plane.

Tape Measure

Tape measures are great to have if you need to figure out the length of something, but be careful with them. If the little piece at the end, the metal piece, is wiggling too much, then your measurements might be a little off because it's worn out.

Sometimes it's best to use a ruler instead of a tape measure as they're more accurate.

Sand Paper

Unless you want your piece to look rough and have rough edges and snags, you're going to need sandpaper. It's best to have very coarse all the way down to the finest grade for woodworking in order to get a smooth, nice finish. Even if you have a belt sander, you're still going to need handheld sandpaper to get into those small crevices.

Power Tools

While you can complete any project with hand tools, sometimes it's nice to have a power tool that can do the job in a fraction of the time it would take you to do it by hand. However, there are some things you should remember when using power tools. Never take off the safety guides and never wear loose clothing or jewelry. You don't want to get caught up in the blades.

Drill

Having an electric drill is going to cut back on your time spent tapping all those holes and drilling the by hand. In addition, you can get attachments that will allow you to drill dowel holes for your joints.

Jigsaw

Jigsaws allow you to cut pretty much any angle or any type of edge you'd like, even circular. However, they're difficult to be accurate with, so be aware that you must have precision when handling the wood and a jigsaw.

Circular Saw

These are for cutting straight edges. A circular saw is built into a table and sticks up out of the table, in most case, although you can get handheld ones. It's best to have a mounted, table version so that you have more control and are less likely to injure yourself.

Belt Sander

If you need to sand off any rough edges, a belt sander is an excellent tool to have in your repertoire. However, you'll still need sandpaper for all those little niches and grooves you'll have to get into with some of the more difficult pieces.

Jointer Planer

Planners are used for when you want to put two pieces of wood together and have them fit flush, such as when you're making a tabletop. While you don't have to own a planer in order to get some of these techniques accomplished, it makes the job a lot easier and the end result usually looks a lot better, too.

There are many other tools out there that you can get hold of for woodworking, but remember that it's best to start with the basics and work your way up to the electrical equipment when you're comfortable with the hand tools.

Chapter 3 – Around the House

Multipurpose Desk, Couch, and Guest Bed

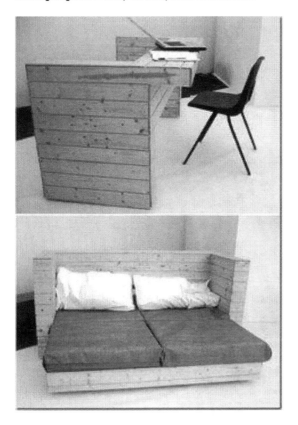

From the side, this piece looks like a normal desk. It's natural wood, yet classy and modern looking, perfect for a sheik office space.

However it can easily double as a great lounge space for relaxing in front of the TV. Unfold it all the way and there is an extra bed for visitors. With this piece of furniture your daytime home office easily turns into a TV room or a guest bedroom at night.

The original in this picture is made with recycled shipping pallets. Thousands of goods are shipped every day on wooden pallets, and, while some of the pallets are recycled, many more are left out to rot. If you ask the right people, pallets can often be obtained for free or at a small price. They can be ripped apart to obtain boards or used as whole pieces.

There are several different types of pallets. The desk frame is made with two close boarded pallets like the one in the picture below turned on end and connected with longer boards across the front.

Lay the two pallets on their long side. Measure the length of your desired desk, cut three boards to length and attach them across the front with screws. If you use wood from another pallet, the boards will already be cut to length and the desk will be the perfect size to slide a pallet bed into.

Cut smaller pieces to fill in all the gaps along the sides of the pallet, and nail some extra boards across the top. Cover the back side of each pallet with boards also to make smooth walls for the bed/couch side of the frame.

Partially deconstruct a third pallet like the one in the picture. Leave three cross slats at the front and the base panels on each end. Attach this frame with screws to the vertical pieces. As before fill in any gaps in the pallet with extra wood. When you are done, sand all the wood smooth with sandpaper or use a wood plane to smooth it. Stain or paint the wood if you would like a more finished look.

Make the bed part as a separate piece. Take two pallets and fill in the underside with extra boards so that they are completely two sided. Lay them down side by side and attach a hinge across the top. This will make it easy to fold the pallets up into a chair or lay them out to make a bed. Cover the pallets with cushions or a folded up futon mattress.

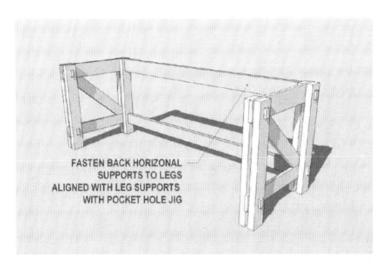

If you don't find good clean pallet wood, or the pallets are the wrong size, this desk/bed can also be made traditional lumber. It's basically the same frame and panel construction that is used to make a door.

Construct a frame for each end of the desk first. The double layered legs and diagonal board in the picture will give the desk more support. Attach the two frames together with boards across the front, and fill in each end with more boards or finished plywood.

What makes the desk/bed convertible is that the desk part will extend in front of the frame instead of across the top like a table. Attach a board to the top of each leg-frame which extend out past the cross panel leaving a 15-20 centimeter overhang. Cover the ledge with more lumber or plywood to make the desk part.

Project Ideas

Cut one pallet in half and use it to mount another pallet to form a low table. This is ideal for standing your television on, as the natural slots in the top pallet can be used for DVD players and digital boxes.

Cut a pallet in half to use as the top of a coffee table, and use the spacing blocks from several others to make the legs. You can use the gap in between the two layers of the top pallet to store magazines or remote controls.

Pole Mounted Shelf:

You can make easily pole mounted floating shelves for your home. These shelves are fixed with the wall. You can choose a specific place for such pole mounted shelves.

Here we choosed a place in front of the window. So you can also pick up any such place where it become easy for you to place and take out the things. You can use these pole mounted shelves for placing books and other things.

Let's learn how to make these shelves!

1. To make these shelves you need to get five wooden boards of appropriate size. Keep the length and width in your mind while buying them. They should neither be too wide or too long. Otherwise they will cover most of your space. Keep them of right size. If they would be too small or less wide then you would not be able to place most of your things. Besides wood you also need three galvanized shin pipes. They will help to secure the shelves in place.

2. After getting the materials you need to make the shelves by using shiny galvanized pipe. Use two pipes at side and one pipe in the middle of these shelves. Moreover secure them in a way that in the bottom they are secure with the ground and from the upper side they are secure with the roof.

But before securing you will be in need of making holes in the wooden boards by using drill machine or any other machine of this nature. After making the holes you will be able to insert the galvanized pipes. While making these shelves don't forget to leave ample space to place most of your things.

In short these are some brilliant DIY woodworking projects to decorate your home walls. You learned in detail that how to decorate your bathroom, small space, room and other parts of your home. These are simple and really very easy steps to make amazing things for your home and surroundings. Walls are often neglected in most of the home but you can go with these projects to decorate them.

Projects Ideas

Wine crates are another excellent source of reclaimed timber. Like pallets, the wood is raw and so will readily take a stain or paint. However, unlike pallets, wine crates have been designed for the transportation of food ideas, and so are perfectly safe for use in kitchens and children's bedrooms. However, wine crates are in greater demand and so you may end up paying for them rather than finding them free of charge.

If you can get hold of some wine crates, they make excellent deep storage drawers for magazine and paperwork. Use boards from a pallet to construct a set of shelves to hold the wine boxes and allow them to slide in and out.

Rusting bathroom shelves:

You can easily make rusting and floating bathroom shelves for your small or large bathroom. If you already have some storage space then its time to remove that. Try this new idea for making rusting bathroom shelves. These wall shelves are not easy to make but also you will be a far much better position to keep most of the things on them. These shelves require very simple material and you can successfully make very easily a wall project like this one.

1. To make this rusting bathroom shelves first you need to decide about some appropriate wall. Choose such a wall that is safe to use. Don't choose a wall that isn't safer. For instance the chances are that most of the thing will fall down. So if they fell down in the flush then it will be a great loss. So decide about the walls that have not such issues.

2. After deciding about the wall next you need to get the material accordingly. If your bathroom is small then you can go vertically. For instance you can make the shelves as shown in the picture. On the other side if you can make a horizontal single shelf as well. But for most of the bathrooms there are simply few things that need to be placed. So don't make your DIY project a complex one.

3. After getting the material like wood you need to cut it in an appropriate way. In this rusting bathroom project we used three shelves of equal size. So you also need to cut the wood accordingly.

4. When you are done with the wood now make some arrangements to secure the shelves. You can make the holes using drill machine and secure the shelves using screws of appropriate size. Keep the equal distance among these shelves otherwise they will look odd.

5. As this is a rusting DIY wood project so we are not going to paint or polish. These shelves look natural and you can place different things on them very easily.

Note: Avoid to place wet things on these wooden shelves.

Projects Ideas

Saw off the bottom eighteen inches of a pallet and use it as a shoe rack. Stand pairs of shoes, toes down, in the gap between the two slats. You can rest this on the ground or even mount it on the wall to save space.

You can also mount a whole pallet on the wall to use as a shoe rock – simple push the pairs of shoes, toe end first, into the gaps in between the slats to hold them off the ground. This is great for small flats where space is limited.

You can make a beautiful display for a table by using four slats (two long, two short) joined together to make an open rectangle. Stand it on its long edge, and drill four holes about the size of a bottle lid at even spaces along the top edge.

Put four jam jars of water under the holes and thread a single flower through the hole into the water. You can adjust the length of the slats and the number of holes to suit your table, or make a taller display and use retro-style fizzy drinks bottles instead of jam jars.

Nursery room book shelves:

You can make this nursery room book shelves anywhere in your home. You can place nursery rhymes on these shelves. They look really beautiful and you can go along with the entire wall by using this project. Let's learn to make this nursery room book shelves.

1. To make these shelves first you need to decide about the wall. Choose any side wall for this purpose.

2. Next to it you need to get five 10 feet long boards. But according to your specific place you can increase or decrease the length of these boards/shelves. If you have relatively small wall then you can keep the size of these boards up to 6 feet.

3. The width of the shelves also matters a lot. If you want to make them more floating then you can make them wide. On the other hand if you don't want to make them floating then you can make the shelves very thin. Most of the people like to keep the thin shelves so that they would be able to keep only the nursery rhymes.

4. After deciding about the length and width you need to secure them with the wall.

5. After securing the shelves appropriately as shown in the picture, you can next paint them. Here paint colour in white is used. This look beautiful when you put the nursery rhymes.

Projects Ideas

Give an old medicine cabinet a new lease of life by cladding the door with waxed or painted pallet slats. This is a great way to cover up an old mirror which has become cracked or discolored.

Bookshelves:

DIY wooden bookshelves are so popular and as a beginner you can take this initiative very easily. If you want to make the study shelves or book shelves for your children then its really not a difficult task. There are many DIY bookshelves plans that you can go with. You can make bookshelves along with the study table. In this design the bookshelves will go vertical. You can also make separate bookshelves on any wall. Some people choose to make bookshelves nearest to their bed. In this way it becomes really easy for them to take out the book.

Another way is that you make the book shelves under the stairs. This is a brilliant idea. Those people having a very small home can go with this type of project. This project will not only save your space but also you will get bookshelves along with study table.

Thus this bookshelf idea will give you a complete and wide study area where you will love to sit and work for longer hours. Let's learn how to work on this project:

1. To make bookshelves under the stair you first need to clear the area. After clearing the area properly you need to paint it. In this way you will get a good place where you will be able to make shelves.

2. Next to it get the wood boards. Here note that you will have to get the wooden boards that are wide enough. In the previous project where you learned to make the nursery rhymes shelves, the width was very low for those shelves. But this project is somewhat different. You can make the separate compartments for placing different types of books. So get the wooden boards that are wide enough.

3. Now make an appropriate design as shown in the picture and secure the boards with the wall.

4. If you want to make a table to place your laptop, PC or other books then you can also make it very easily. For this purpose you will be in need to get the wide enough boards and secure them properly.

5. When you are done with the bookshelves and table, paint them in appropriate colour. When its dry you can place your books and other materials. In this way you will get a well decorated and simple study area under the stairs.

Projects Ideas

Stack up a few of the spacer blocks that hold the slats apart and glue them together to make a lamp base. You can offset the blocks (rather than lining them up square) to give the lamp base more interest.

Pallet shelves:

Usually people love to work with pallets. The main reason is that they come in appropriate size and working with them is relatively easy. People are using wooden pallets in most of the DIY projects and applying them to make shelves is really a good idea.

You can make amazing pallet shelves for keeping decorative items, pictures and books. Pallet projects are also used in kitchen and bathrooms. So after getting a basic idea you can make pallet shelves to decorate the walls of your home. Moreover pallet garden shelves are also very popular. But here you will learn to make pallet shelves to decorate your room.

1. To make the pallet shelves first you need to get the pallets of appropriate size. According to the size of shelves you can get the shelves. For the small space home you can go vertically with these pallets.

2. Decide a corner wall or any other wall for making shelves.

3. After that arrange the pallets to make appropriate shelves. You can also get a design for making wall shelves. In this way you will be able to find that how much and what type of material you will need.

4. You need to get nails and screws to fix the shelves.

5. After fixing the shelves you can paint them in appropriate colour. If you are using them for your children then you can use some bright colours.

6. When the paint is dry you can then place your important things on these shelves.

Projects Ideas

Split off one side of a pallet, leaving one large flat side in tact with the spacer bars still on. Remove the spacer bars from an identically sized pallet and add to the first side to make a series of narrow shelves. Mount this on the wall and use as a spice rack.

Chapter 4 – In the Garden

Projects Ideas

Wood pallets nailed to a wall make an ideal surface for climbing plants (such as clematis or wisteria) to train up. This is easier and more attractive than stringing wires across a surface and then painstakingly encouraging the tendrils to grown across them.

Fill a pallet with earth and stand it on its side against a wall. Plant strawberry plants in the gaps between the slats, not forgetting the sides.

Use pallets on their sides to create dividers or fences. Drive a stake into the ground to support the pallet and nail or cable tie them together. The advantage of using pallets is that the fence can easily be moved as well as being a good surface for climbing plants to grow up.

The slats from Pallets are also the ideal height for making a picket fence. If you want to complete the look, angle the end of each slat into a point.

The slats from a pallet make a great decking-style path across lawns.

Two pallets joined together in an L-shape can be used as a bike rack. Slot the front wheel of each bike into the gap between the slats to save space in your garage and make each bike more accessible.

Saw off the bottom eighteen inches of a pallet and turn the resultant shelf into a window box.

The slats from a pallet make a great decking-style path across lawns.

Use a lot of pallets to make a tunnel or arch. Train vines up it to provide a Mediterranean-style shaded area for your patio or back yard.

Use four pallets on their ends to make a compost heap container. The wooden slats allow good drainage and circulation of air to help your garden waste and vegetable peelings biodegrade faster.

Deconstruct a few wooden pallets and use the planks to make a raised bed. Remember to add drainage clinker or gravel to the bottom before you add your topsoil or compost to aid drainage. Raised beds are ideal if your garden has poor soil, or if you find bending difficult. They also add interest to your garden layout by letting you have plants on a variety of levels.

DIY Wood Futon

This futon frame is made with pine lumber, screws, and bolts with wing nuts. This is an incredible savings over market costs, and you'll have a nice couch that can fold out and double as a guest bed.

The frame is made from three separate pieces of wood attached with screws that rotate so that the back can be folded up or be lain out flat. Twelve longer cross planks make the surface where the mattress will sit.

This excellent <u>design</u> is by VV Board on *Instructorless*. The length for the parallel wood pieces that make up the base are very exact to ensure that the futon will fold up as needed.

You will need 2 boards 77 centimeters by 7 centimeters, 2 boards 70 centimeters by 7 centimeters, and 2 boards 69 centimeters by 7 centimeters. All wood should be 2 centimeters thick. Additionally, you will need 12 long planks 120 centimeters by 9.5 centimeters, for the top cross slats.

You will also need four 6 millimeter bolts at least 5 centimeters long with nuts to match and at least 22 regular sized wood screws to attach the top planks.

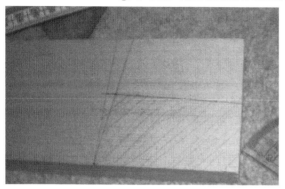

Start with the smallest 69 x 7 centimeter planks. These will make the far end of the futon, the extra part that hangs down the back when it is folded into a couch. Taper 1 end by measuring 2 centimeters in and 2 centimeters down on the wood.

Draw a straight line connecting these two points and cut out the wood. Drill a 6 millimeter hole for the bolt in the same end of the wood. Measure down 3 centimeters and drill the hole exactly in the middle of the board. Drill all the way through the wood.

Cut a small wedge out of the other end of the boards, as shown in the picture. Measure 8.5 centimeters down and draw a perpendicular line. Measure a 7 degree angle up from this line and draw a 3.7 centimeter long line from the edge into the center of the board. From this point measure a 90 degree angle toward the top of the board and draw another line straight up. Cut out this angle, which is just slightly acute. This will make a ledge which can rest on the bottom boards when the bed is folded up so that the back of the couch will be supported.

Taper one end of the medium 70 x 7 centimeter boards in the same way as the small ones. Measure 2 centimeters in and down, draw a line between the two points and cut out the corresponding triangle on each side. Measure 3 centimeters down from the top of the board and drill a hole exactly in the center of board.

At the other end, measure 5 centimeters down and 1.5 centimeters in. Mark the point and drill a 6 millimeter hole here. On this end cut off just one corner, the corner opposite the drill hole. Measure 2.5 centimeters in and down and cut off the corner along the triangular line between the two points. These boards will form the middle section of the futon.

On the largest of the base boards, the 77 x 7 centimeter pieces, drill a hole in only one end. Measure 16.5 centimeters down and 1.5 centimeters in to mark the place for the hole. Taper 1 side of the board on the same end as this hole in a similar way to the medium boards. Choose the corner directly opposite the hole, measure 3.5 centimeters in and 3.5 centimeters down and cut off this triangle. This picture demonstrates exactly what the boards should look like when they are all finished.

The two tapered ends of the small and medium boards will align, with the smallest boards on the outside and a bolt through both drill holes. The two off-center drill holes and cut triangle on the medium and largest boards will align, with the longer boards on the outside and another bolt through both drill holes. The untouched ends of the longer boards will rest on the floor, while the notched ends of the smallest boards will rest on the ends of the longer boards when the futon is folded into a couch.

Make screw holes on the long cross planks also. On 7 of the planks, measure 15 centimeters down on each end. Mark the midpoint of the board and measure 2 centimeters on either side of the midpoint to mark the place to drill (4 holes on each board.) On 4 of the planks measure 17 centimeters down and drill a hole 2 centimeters on either side of the midpoint (4 holes on each board.) On 1 plank just make 2 holes, 1 on each end, 15 centimeters down in the middle of the board.

On the shortest boards, (69 x 7 centimeters) make 8 screw holes to attach 4 cross boards. Start 8.5 centimeters from the tapered end to mark the first hole. Mark the second drill-hole 4 centimeters from the first (all the holes should be exactly in the center of the boards on the narrowest side.) Measure 13.5 centimeters to drill the next hole and another 4 centimeters to drill a hole for the second side of the board. Make holes for 2 more boards like with the first hole at 13.5 centimeters and the second 4 centimeters away (this matches the 4 centimeters between the two holes on the cross planks.)

Make similar holes for 4 cross planks on the medium boards. Start the first hole 14.5 centimeters from the end with the single corner cut off and the off-center drill hole. Make the second hole 4 centimeters from the first. Measure 11 centimeters between boards for the next hole and another 4 centimeters for the other side of the board. Add holes for two more boards at equal intervals.

On the longer boards (77 x 7 centimeters) measure 3 centimeters in from the square end to make a drill hole. This is where the board with the single hole will be attached. From this mark, measure 13.5 centimeters to mark the second hole. Measure 4 centimeters to mark the hole for the second side of the board.

Measure 12.5 centimeters between boards for the next hole and another 4 centimeters to make a hole for the other side of the board. Add holes for one more board at a 12.5 centimeter interval from the last board.

The holes on the long cross planks will need to extend all the way through the board. On the smaller parallel boards they will just need to extend about 2 centimeters into the wood. The first 7 long planks with the holes 15 centimeters in will go on the small and longer boards. The 4 planks with the holes 17 centimeters down will go into the medium boards (remember these are the boards on the inside!) The single plank with only two holes goes on the long boards next to the square end.

Before assembling sand all the pieces to make them smoother. Attach the cross planks using an electric screwdriver. Once the cross planks are attached, assemble the frame pieces using the long bolts with a nut on each end. Top the frame with a futon mattress.

It's possible to adjust this design to fit you space just by cutting the long cross-planks in half and keeping all the measurements for the parallel base boards the same. Make a chair sized futon to add an extra cot sized bed if that design fits better with your apartment.

Projects Ideas

Cut four pallets down the centre and stack together to create a simple outdoor bench.

Cut a pallet into four squares and stack up to make a matching stool.

Two pallets propped like a house of cards make the ideal starting structure for a hen coop. You will need to use additional pallet wood to create a back and a front, with a hinged door for the hens to be let in and out. Build perches and roosting boxes inside and add clean straw for nesting. Place the hen house onto another pallet to keep it off the damp, cold ground and allow the circulation of air.

If you can source a wooden cable drum, this makes an excellent garden table without any need for adaptation. Sand off any rough edges and treat the wood with a non-toxic finish to protect it from the elements.

Chapter 5 – In the Garage

Projects Ideas

If you have a rabbit hutch, you may find yourself bringing the rabbits in to the garage through the colder months. You should never place the hutch directly onto a concrete floor, as this can get very cold. Use a pallet to insulate the hutch from the ground, and make sure you place the hutch out of any drafts.

A pallet nailed to a wall in the garage makes a great surface to hang tools. Hammer in nails to support tools without hooks. This keeps them safe, away from damp, and allows you to see at a glance if any are missing.

The bottom twelve inches of a pallet can be sawn off and turned into a toolbox or project box. It is ideal for keeping everything you need for a particular project – tools, tins of paint, glue, string, etc – together in one place.

Make a feeding station for your large pet dog by using the planks from a pallet to construct a hinged box about twelve inches high. Use the interior to store your pet's food, and cut a circular hole in the lid big enough to slot in your pet's feeding bowl.

This will make it easier for the dog to eat (by raising their bowl off the ground) as well as stopping the bowl from sliding around. For this project, it is best to use brand new pallets which you are sure have not been exposed to harmful chemicals.

Use a pallet screen to hide an unsightly feature, such as a water tank or wheelie bins.

Use the slats to construct shelves. Not only do you have the top surface of the shelf to stand items on, but you can also nail the lids of jam jars along the bottom edge. When the jar is screwed in to its lid, it will hang securely below the shelf, allowing you to see at a glance what it contains. Use these jars to store nails, screws and other small items.

Use short lengths of slats to make labels and signs for your outside space. You can use paint, permanent marker (make sure you seal the sign with varnish or wax) or even burn the information into the wood using a hot iron.

If you have heavy equipment that you need to move regularly (such as a gas canister, for example) then fit four sturdy wheels, one on each corner. Stand the heavy item on the pallet to make it easier to move about.

You can use the planks from pallets to make a garden shed. Find a simple design from the internet and make sure that you pay attention to the roof construction and waterproofing. Due to the short nature of the planks, it is easier to make a small shed that a large one – use it for storing wood or bikes to keep them out of the rain.

If you have a large garage with an overhead storage area, you can stack up pallets in groups of two to make a staircase. Make sure you brace it securely against the wall and support it from underneath so that it is safe to take your weight.

Chapter 4 – Storage and Decoration Ideas

DIY DVD Bookshelf:

This is a DVD bookshelf but you can place so many other things on it as well. For the larger home this DVD bookshelf idea is really great and easy. You can amazingly place your books and other things on these DVD bookshelves. On the one hand your books will remain on one place while on the other side you will decorate you wall in an incredible way. These are three DVD bookshelves with same size and style to décor your wall. Let's learn how to make these DVD bookshelves!

1. To make these DVD bookshelves first you need to get three large and wide boards. Moreover you will need 12 small wooden boards that will serve as shelves.

2. After getting the wooden boards you need to paint them. Here we painted in blue but you can also paint them in any colour of your choice. When the paint is dry then move to the next step.

3. The next step is to secure the shelves with the large wooden board as shown in the picture. Go for the rest of two shelves in the same way.

4. When you are done with the shelves they are now in a position to secure with the wall. Use drill machine to make holes and then use screws to secure these shelves with the walls.

5. If you notice carefully we also used vertical wooden boards in the upper and lower shelves. These boards helps the books to stand. On the top most shelf you can place the picture or other decorative items as well.
Thus this is an amazing DIY woodworking DVD bookshelf project to decorate your walls.

1. Choose a plank of pallet wood which has particularly nice markings or aging. Sand lightly and apply several coats of beeswax to bring out the grain of the wood. Use the board to mount several iron hooks and use as a coat rack in the hall.

2. Cut off the bottom twelve inches of several pallets and mount them on the wall to use as wine racks. Choose somewhere cool, dry and away from direct sunlight and heat sources if you intend to store the wine on a long-term basis.

Multipurpose Closet Space

Put several different projects together to turn a small, not very useful closet into a multipurpose storage space or even an extra room. There are many ways to expand on existing space using very simple woodworking projects as well as imagination.

The very simplest way to recreate a closet is just to add shelves. These shelves are made with three boards stapled together. They are supported with cross boards nailed onto the wall just underneath each shelf. This can also be accomplished with a metal bracket support. A dowel rod suspended from a shelf can create an extra hanging rack if your closet lacks one.

Turning a Closet into an Office Space

This is an ingenious project which can create a whole new room in your house. If you have a large closet, turn it into a home office which packs away as if it never existed. There are several project which can accomplish this.

If your closet has a sliding door, you will need to remove it and replace it with hinged doors that open out like the picture. Buy the doors, locate recycled doors (sometimes this is possible through Habitat for Humanity) or make you own using a basic frame and panel construction. This won't need to be a high security exterior door. A panel of ¾inch (19 millimeter) plywood supported with a frame and covered with pine boards can make a great <u>rustic door</u>.

Paint the wood to match. The difference in coloring between the interior closet walls and the exterior room wall makes the cubby hole look even more like a separate room. Run a grove down the back of each door and attach them to the wall with hinges.

Make a bulletin board to hand on the back of the door. Construct a wooden frame, and fill the interior door panels with cork or hole board so that you can hang files, CD's or more storage hooks. This is also a great place to put cards and children's art work.

Decorate the inside of the closet as if it were a room. Matching paint and wallpaper designs will make the look more attractive and open. Make shelves along the back wall for extra storage. You can build a desk out of file cabinets like the picture, or make your own wooden desk to fit the space, as was described in the last chapter.

Turning a Closet Door into a Bookshelf

This is an amazing design for a closet door. It's basically a plywood box construction just like the cabinet in Chapter 3 with as many shelves as you want for books or decorative cabinet areas. Use lazy Susan hinges to open and close the door since there will be a lot of weight. You may even want to put wheels on the bottom of the bookcase so that it will open and close more easily.

Tiny Hidden Storage Spaces

There are many ways to create hidden storage space. This is a picture with a hidden compartment which can be used to store medication, jewelry or other personal items. Even without a lock, this is a safer space since a thief will be less likely to notice it.

This is a good place to use some finer wood and more intricate technique. Chisel groves into the four box pieces so that they fit together and slide in another board for the backing. Use tiny hinges to attach the door so they won't be too visible. Insert a mirror into the inside of the door to make it even more multipurpose. Attach your favorite picture reproduction to the outside. You can even paint the picture yourself or ask an artist friend.

This is another design for as similar hidden storage space. This time the compartment is actually recessed back into the wall. Most people don't have this type of space built into their house or apartment, but it's easy enough to insert into a drywall partition with a bit of space behind.

Build a small cabinet to size complete with shelves for storing wine.Slide it into the space and secure it to the drywall. The shelf at the front hinges up to help keep the wine from falling out. With the two sided painting, it makes a lovely art piece open or shut.

DIY triangle wall shelf:

To decorate your home walls you can also go for this project. This DIY triangle wall shelf project is really great and you can easily work on it. By following just few steps you can make this project for your home. There are several ways to accomplish this project and you can choose anyone of your choice that you think is easier. Let's learn how to make this shelf!

1. To make this triangular shelf you need some materials like lumber, glue, tape measure, brand nailer and meter saw. After getting these materials you can further start working on this project.

2. As discussed there are several ways to complete a project like this one or similar to this one. I will here suggest you to make 6 triangles to make these triangular shelves.

3. Use the measuring tape and cut the lumber in equal sized to make a perfect triangle as shown in the picture.

4. After that use wood glue and secure the wood parts.

5. Next to it you need to join all the triangles with each other to make a perfect shelf as shown in the picture. You can secure it with the wall using screws.

In short these are some of the DIY woodworking shelf projects that you can use for your home to décor the walls. These are easy and incredible shelf projects that are quite useful for the beginners. You can learn to make bookshelves while going vertical, you can make triangular shelves for placing books and decorative items, you can make hexagonal shelves for your garage and so on. Thus you can go with any of the above mentioned project to decorate your home walls.

Projects Ideas

3. Use the planking from several pallets to clad a wall. Offset the lengths to break up the line of the join and choose planks which have few or no knot or nail holes. This makes a very striking feature wall in a bedroom or bathroom.

4. Three short planks held together at both sides by another small plank of wood makes a useful tray. Drill two holes through each side and thread through twine or ribbon to make easy-to-carry handles.

5. Mount a pallet on the wall of your kitchen and use butcher's hooks to hang utensils, pots and pans. You can also hang a pallet flat from your ceiling and use for more overhead storage of pans, or as a drying rack for laundry.

Entertainment Shelves:

You can easily make entertainment shelves for your home. Your children often want entertainment shelves for their rooms. You can make such shelves for them in this way. These are very good type of shelves and you can move them anywhere in your home. But remember that these shelves need to place with the walls.

Without wall you can't place your most of things. They will otherwise drop/fall because no other wooden board is used in the back of the shelves. These entertainment shelves are made in three portions. The middle one is smaller while the two shelves at the side are somewhat in larger size. In these entertainment shelves galvanized rods/pipes are also used. You can use these entertainment shelves for placing different things. Moreover books can also be placed on such shelves.

Let's now learn that how to make these entertainment shelves!

6. To make these entertainment shelves you first need to get the wood and galvanized pipes. Get 16 wooden boards and 8 galvanized pipes. Make sure that the wooden boards are of equal size. In this way they will help in proper alignment of the shelves. Moreover the galvanized pipes should also be in right and equal size. Because they will help in balancing of the shelves.

7. After getting the materials to make entertainment shelves, next you need to secure them properly. When you are done with it you can place different things on these shelves.

8. A pallet with the spacer blocks removed leaves you with two flat grids of wooden slats. These make a decorative headboard for a double bed, and can be painted to match the walls or waxed and left natural.

9. You can use the same technique to make a jewelry display rack. Mount the flat side of the pallet on the wall, and add hooks to hang earrings, necklaces and bracelets. This not only makes an attractive display, but will keep your jewelry from becoming tangled and make sure you can see at a glance all your different pieces.

10. Use the slats to make a picture frame. This works best for large, bold pictures with an outdoor or natural theme.

11. Don't forget the spacer blocks from the pallets. Use a large drill bit to carve out a hole about half an inch deep in the centre of a square block, and use it as a tea light holder.

12. A long block can make an attractive table decorative. Using a chisel, carefully carve out a channel in the centre of the block and fill it with coloured glass pebbles, shells you have collected or even beads and buttons.

Entryway shelf:

As a beginner you can easily make this entryway shelf for your room. This shelf has so many advantages and you can place your most of things on this shelf. First of all this shelf can be used to hang your most of the things such as shoulder bags, hats and coats. Secondly on the top of this shelf you can place some other things like pictures, vase and other decorative items etc. So learning to make this shelf is you good idea. On one side you will be able to clutter most of the things while on the other side it will look very beautiful in your room. Let's learn how to make this entryway shelf!

13. To make this entryway shelf you need very few materials. Such as you need hooks, wood, paint, some screws and a drill machine.
14. After getting the materials cut and join the wooden parts in the same way as shown in the picture.
15. Next to it paint the back, sides, top and bottom portion of the wood. But don't paint the front portion. The reason is that when you will use the screws and studs they will look ugly.
16. When you are done with the paint next you need to secure the shelf with the wall. Use drill machine to make three large pilot sized holes to secure the screws. Also make some small holes with drill machine to secure the hooks.

17. After securing the shelf with the wall you next need to paint the front part of it that you left earlier. Paint in a way that screws don't appear.
18. Next you need to secure the hooks. Here we got 10 hooks and now you need to secure them in a proper line. In this way your this DIY entryway project is complete and you can hang and place your different things on it.

Garage shelves:

Wooden shelves are not only used for indoors but also you can use them for outdoors as well. This is a very simple wooden wall shelf project that can be used for your garage wall. If you want to use the wood in really an amazing way then going for this wood project can prove very vital for you. This project can be accomplished by using wooden pallets or small pieces of wood. Let's learn that how to work on this project!

19. First of all you need to locate an empty wall in your garage. After locating the wall you need to start work on this DIY shelf project.
20. According to the size of your wall you can increase or decrease the size of these hexagonal shaped shelves. As shown in the picture we used two shelves. The left one with the larger size while the right and upper one with the smaller size. If you have quite bigger wall then you can add more shelves as well.
21. To make these garage shelves you need wooden boards of small and equal sized as shown in the picture. For each shelf you will need to have six wooden boards.
22. After getting the boards secure them with the glue and nails. When the shelf is complete, mount it on the wall and then place the pots on it. In the same manner you can make other shelves as well. If you want to give any other shape to your garage shelves then still you can give. This garage shelf idea is very basic and you can further make your mind for difficult and complicated projects in this way.
23. Paint slats with blackboard paint and use it as a message board for the family to keep a record of items for the shopping list, important jobs and phone messages.

Conclusion

We hope you have enjoyed this guide to reusing pallets inside and outside your home. As you can see, we have chosen some of the simplest projects for beginners, but once you are familiar with what a pallet can provide, you may feel confident enough to undertake bigger and more ambitious projects. Almost anything that can be made of wood can be made from pallets; it is just a question of adapting the project to the limitations of the material.

In fact, you may find that your only limitation is the number of pallets you can get your hands on – this trend for upcycling pallets is growing rapidly in popularity, as other people cotton on to this free (or very cheap) source of materials. Get in and take your claim!

Made in the USA
Lexington, KY
25 February 2019